Older than the Dinosaurs

THE ORIGIN AND RISE
OF THE MAMMALS

Older than the Dinosaurs

The Origin and Rise of the Mammals

By Edward R. Ricciuti

Illustrated by Edward Malsberg

Thomas Y. Crowell • New York

LIBRARY OF CONGRESS CATALOGING IN PUBLICATION DATA

Ricciuti, Edward R. Older than the dinosaurs.

SUMMARY: Discusses the evolution and development
of mammals following the age of the giant reptiles.
1. Mammals, Fossil—Juvenile literature.
[1. Mammals, Fossil. 2. Prehistoric animals]
I. Malsberg, Edward.   II. Title.
QE881.R53   569   77-26606
ISBN 0-690-01328-0   ISBN 0-690-03879-8 lib. bdg.
10 9 8 7 6 5 4 3 2 1
FIRST EDITION

For Donny Nelson, who would have been champ

Contents

Older than the Dinosaurs

THE ORIGIN AND RISE OF THE MAMMALS

GEOLOGICAL TIME SCALE

Read from Bottom to Top.

Eras	Time Periods Rock Systems	Time Epochs Rock Series *time span millions of years*	*millions of years ago*	Life Forms
Cenozoic	Quaternary	Recent / Pleistocene	1	Rise and dominance of man.
	Upper Tertiary	Pliocene / Miocene 70	25	Modern animals and plants.
	Lower Tertiary	Oligocene / Eocene / Paleocene	70	Rapid development of modern mammals, insects, and plants.
Mesozoic	Upper Cretaceous	65		Primitive mammals; last dinosaurs.
	Lower Cretaceous		135	Rise of flowering plants.
	Jurassic	45	180	First birds, first mammals. Diversification of reptiles; climax of ammonites; coniferous trees.
	Triassic	40	220	Rise of dinosaurs; cycadlike plants; bony fishes.
Paleozoic	Permian	50	270	Rise of reptiles. Modern insects. Last of many plant and animal groups.
	Pennsylvanian ⎱ Carboniferous	80		First reptiles. Amphibians; primitive insects; seed ferns; primitive conifers.
	Mississippian ⎰		350	Climax of shell-crushing sharks.
	Devonian	50	400	First amphibians, first land snails. Primitive land plants. Climax of brachiopods.
	Silurian	40	440	First traces of land life. Scorpions. First lungfish. Widespread coral reefs.
	Ordovician	60	500	First fish. Climax of trilobites. First appearance of many marine invertebrates.
	Cambrian	100	600	First marine invertebrates, including trilobites.
	Precambrian			First signs of life. Algae.

Age of Oldest Dated Rocks: About 3,000,000,000 yrs.

In the Days
Before the Dinosaurs

The forest resembles an unbroken wall of green, rising high above the soggy ground into a hot sky the color of tarnished brass. Amidst the tangle of greenery grow trees that tower 150 feet over the pools of syrupy, yellow water on the forest floor. They are strange trees, indeed. Some have trunks that appear jointed and end in tufted crowns. Others resemble giant brushes, with handles planted in the earth. Still others are topped by feathery fronds, which arch out from their trunks, then droop toward the ground.

You would see such a forest if somehow you could travel back in time to the period known as the Carboniferous, which ended

270 million years ago. The forests of that period are known as "coal forests," because the partly decayed remains of their vegetation were eventually buried under tremendous pressure and changed to coal. Some coal still bears the imprints, or fossils, of the ancient plants that made it.

The huge trees of the coal forest certainly would seem strange, but some of them—the one described above, for example—might also look slightly familiar. That would be because they are giant forms of plants still living today, such as the small horsetails, club mosses, and ferns that grow in damp woodlands and moist corners of city parks.

Another thing that would be strange about the coal forest is that no birds would be calling. You might hear the wind whispering in the foliage, perhaps the spatter of rain, and the buzzing of insects—but not a single bird. The first birds would not appear until more than 100 million years after the Carboniferous period ended.

Dinosaurs also did not appear until long after the coal forests had vanished. But a number of other groups of reptiles inhabited these steaming jungles. One group is known as the pelycosaurs. They arose at the end of the Carboniferous period and really began to thrive in the Permian, which followed it. One well-known pelycosaur was called *Dimetrodon*, the "finback" or "sail reptile." Ten feet long, with huge head and toothy jaws, *Dimetro-*

Dimetrodon

Sphenacodon

Eryops

don carried a great ribbed fin, or sail, atop its back. Another big pelycosaur, called *Sphenacodon*, looked like *Dimetrodon* but without the huge sail.

During the Permian, *Sphenacodon*, or something quite like it, gave rise to a new line of reptiles called therapsids. That occurred about 250 million years ago. The therapsids lasted for 50 million years. About the time the dinosaurs began to flourish, the last therapsids disappeared. Before they vanished, however, the therapsids in turn produced another new group of creatures. But this new group was not included in the class of reptiles. It was an entirely different class of animals—the mammals. This is the class that includes humans, and that has dominated the world since the age of reptiles ended about 70 million years ago.

The story of the origin and rise of the mammals is a tale older than the dinosaurs. But it remains important today. Not only is it our story, since we ourselves are mammals, but it can help us understand much about the problems that many animals face today in trying to survive. The story begins long before there were any humans on earth, when wild animals existed in a purely natural state. But for many, many years, this has been far from the case. The influence of expanding human populations and technology has had such an impact on the natural scheme of things that the old rules in the game of survival no longer apply.

In Africa, for example, grasslands that since prehistoric times have supported great herds of game animals and the flesh eaters that prey upon them are being changed to cattle ranches and farms. There is little or no room in such places for game, and certainly not for lions. Farmers trying to feed their families have planted their crops on the ancestral feeding grounds of elephants. When the elephants return there to feed, they destroy the crops, and their death, in turn, is demanded by the farmers. But who can blame the farmers when their families are hungry?

Many people in the western United States, especially cattle ranchers, feel there is no place below the Canadian border for the grizzly bear. Grizzlies sometimes attack livestock. Moreover, the last wildernesses left to the grizzly are being invaded by campers, skiers, and other recreation seekers. Grizzlies can be touchy about people and dangerous to meet unexpectedly. A number of people have been killed or injured by the bears. If the grizzly is to survive, it needs lots of room between itself and civilization, and the wide open spaces are almost gone.

The American bison was caught in the same squeeze as the grizzly. Once 60 million bison roamed the vast western prairies and plains. Today the only bison that remain—about 30 thousand of them—are restricted to wildlife refuges, parks, and preserves. The boundless open spaces that once supported them have been cut up and converted into grazing land, wheat fields, and corn-fields. Never again, although they have been saved from extinction, will the bison exist in great numbers, because the unlimited open land they needed to survive in immense herds has gone.

The bison and grizzly along with other large mammals, such as the rhinoceros, elephant, and tiger, are known to have existed since late in what we term "prehistoric times." They originated in a world vastly different from the one in which we live today. There is no way that on their own they can keep up with the changes in the environment caused by humans and their activities. They are in a very real sense yesterday's animals.

If these creatures are to be kept from extinction, we need to know from whence they came and what they need to survive. In this sense, to understand the future, we must understand the past. A good place to begin to examine the past history of the mammals is in the ancient coal forests during the millions of years in which the Carboniferous period was drawing to a close, and the Permian was dawning.

During the Carboniferous, plant life thrived as never before or since. Vast swampy forests covered most of the land. The world was generally hot and humid, as in much of the tropics today. Temperatures were regular. Climate changed little from one part of the world to another, and from one season to the next. The conditions were excellent for the earliest reptiles. They first appeared in the second half of the Carboniferous, descending from the amphibians—smooth-skinned, cold-blooded creatures that begin life in the water.

The earliest reptiles were rather similar to their amphibian ancestors. But there were some important differences between them. Amphibian eggs typically survive only in water. Reptile eggs, on the other hand, have a tough shell that holds in moisture, and they therefore will survive when deposited on land. After hatching, young amphibians go through a tadpole, water-breathing stage, before they take on adult form and breathe air. Young reptiles are already air-breathing, smaller editions of the adults at the moment of hatching or, in a few cases, of birth. A small number of snakes and lizards bear living young, but they were the last reptiles to appear, and are the most advanced of all.

The first known reptiles were the cotylosaurs. Very early in their history they branched out in two directions. One branch became the main line of reptilian evolution. Eventually it led to such varied reptiles as dinosaurs, turtles, crocodilians, snakes, and lizards. It also led to the birds. The other line led to the pelycosaurs, and then through the therapsids to the mammals.

The pelycosaurs were the first really big reptiles. Included among them are *Dimetrodon* and *Sphenacodon*, two terrors who prowled the dank forests, killing and eating other reptiles, as well as amphibians. Even the huge amphibian *Eryops*, as big as a man and fierce in its own right, could not withstand them. *Dimetrodon* and *Sphenacodon* were the dominant land animals of the early Permian period, the dawn of the age of reptiles, the time these creatures were the dominant life on land.

It is difficult to imagine that the pelycosaurs belonged to the line that eventually led to the mammals. They were scaly, squat, and slow, and like other reptiles they were cold-blooded. That is, the temperature of their bodies rose or dropped depending on how hot or cold it was around them. For warmth, they had to bask in the sun, or lie on a warm rock. To cool off, they had to go into a cave, the shade, or the water. Reptiles spend much of the time trying to regulate their body temperature.

At the same time, however, the pelycosaurs had a few characteristics that were somewhat like mammals. In fact, they and their descendants, the therapsids, are known as the "mammal-like reptiles." One mammal-like trait obvious in *Sphenacodon* and *Dimetrodon* was the enlarged canine teeth they used to stab prey. The teeth in the mouths of most reptiles are all the same shape and size; the fangs of venomous snakes are an exception. Reptiles do not chew food, but usually gulp it down whole or in chunks. A reptile uses its teeth merely to grab food, and perhaps tear it into pieces small enough to swallow. But a mammal usually has several different types of teeth in its jaws for specialized jobs such as chewing, cutting, or grinding. The enlarged canines of some pelycosaurs were a step in this direction.

The pelycosaurs had an especially powerful bite, because of an opening in the skull behind each ear that allowed the jaw muscles to bulge outward. This, too, is a trait of mammals. Except for the pelycocaurs and therapsids, no other reptiles have ever possessed it. As time passed, the therapsids, particularly, developed more and more mammal-like traits. Eventually they reached the border-line between reptiles and mammals.

Mammals differ from reptiles in many ways that are quite obvious. Mammals are warm-blooded, which means that their body temperature is maintained internally, at a steady level. The cells of a mammal's body are like tiny furnaces, burning nutrients for fuel and generating heat. A mammal is able to conserve the heat produced by its body because the hair covering it—only mammals have hair—serves as insulation. Under normal conditions, therefore, a healthy mammal can keep its internal temperature at the proper level—as long as it has enough food to fuel its cellular furnaces.

Mammals and reptiles differ also in the way they treat their young. Reptiles provide little or no care for their offspring, although a few, such as the female alligator, will sometimes protect eggs and hatchlings. Mammals not only provide considerable care

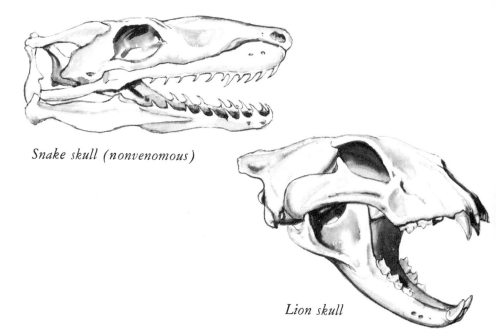

Snake skull (nonvenomous)

Lion skull

for their young, but they nourish them on mother's milk, produced by means of another unique mammalian feature—mammary glands.

There are, of course, many major differences in the body structure of mammals and reptiles. The nostrils of most reptiles, for instance, open directly into the mouth. The nasal and oral passages of mammals (and of the crocodilians alone among reptiles), on the other hand, are separated by a structure called the secondary palate. It serves a very important function in mammals, as we shall see later in this chapter.

When it comes to deciding whether an animal is a mammal or a reptile, however, scientists rely on only one characteristic—the structure of the lower jaw. A reptile's lower jaw is made up of several bones, joined by connective tissue. In the front is the dentary, which carries all the lower teeth. The bone most to the rear is the articular. It touches the skull, where it meets a bone called the quadrate to form the jaw joint.

Mammals have a lower-jaw structure more suited to their way of life. The only bone in the lower jaw of a mammal is the one that bears the teeth, the dentary. Because it goes all the way from front to rear, there is more room on it for the many different types of teeth a mammal needs. Moreover, a single jawbone is stronger than one of several bones linked together. Mammals need strong jaws for such jobs as cracking open bones and grinding up tough vegetable matter. The jaw joint of a mammal is not formed by the articular and quadrate bones, but by the dentary and by a bone on the side of the skull called the squamosal. Scientists consider any animal with a lower jaw composed only of the dentary, joined to the skull at the squamosal, as a mammal.

What about the articular and quadrate bones in mammals? Mammals have these two bones, but in a very different form and place than reptiles do, and they also serve a very different purpose. The articular and quadrate of mammals are in the middle ear. The articular bone serves as the malleus, or hammer. The quadrate is the incus, or anvil. They work together to transmit sound from the eardrum to the inner ear.

Sphenacodon and *Dimetrodon* had typical reptilian jaws. But during the development of the later mammal-like reptiles, the dentary began to grow larger. Eventually it grew so much that it pushed aside the other bones of the lower jaw. The last mammal-like reptiles had a dentary that was so large it reached the skull. Some of them had the dentary-squamosal jaw joint in front, and the old articular-quadrate joint hidden behind it.

Such alterations took enormous amounts of time, millions upon millions of years. But ever so surely the traits that we recognize as belonging to the mammals appeared increasingly in the line that had begun with the pelycosaurs.

While the mammal-like reptiles were slowly changing, so was the earth's environment. The continents of the Carboniferous were made up mostly of low, flat jungles. The climate also had been monotonous—like an endless, hot, humid summer. But after the beginning of the Permian, the earth began to stir. Mountains rose. Snowstorms swirled over the temperate zones. The tropics were sometimes wet, sometimes desert-dry.

When there are major changes in the environment, pressure to change is also put upon the species living within it. If the species do not develop characteristics that will enable them to survive in the face of change, they will vanish. Such traits for survival are called adaptations. They develop only slowly, in the course of generations, through the process of evolution. The hoof that helps a horse to run swiftly over the grasslands, the instinct that enables wolves to hunt as a pack—these are examples of adaptations to changes in environment.

The conditions of the later Permian were too much for *Dimetrodon* and *Sphenacodon*. They had originated in a world where forest steamed in endless soggy heat for millions of years. Perhaps, therefore, *Dimetrodon* and *Sphenacodon* could not survive in a climate that varied in humidity and temperature. By the late Permian, they were gone, and so were most of the other pelycosaurs. The therapsids, however, were already on the scene— still reptiles, but much more mammal-like than the pelycosaurs. From the widespread areas where their fossils have been found, it seems that the therapsids were able to exist under a varied range of conditions. Their bones have been discovered in places as far apart as the Soviet Union and South Africa.

Therapsids—it is a name strange to many people, yet for 50 million years, possibly five times the period humanity has existed, therapsids ruled the earth. There were therapsids who ate plants, and other therapsids who ate the plant eaters. There were therapsids smaller than squirrels, and others the size of a moose. True giants had not yet appeared among the land animals, although there were great creatures in the sea.

The major group of plant-eating therapsids were the anomodonts, of which there were many different kinds. They varied in size from being among the smallest to the largest therapsids. Many had teeth suited for rooting and digging. Some had two large tusks pointing downward from the upper jaw, which could be used to dig up vegetation, especially from swamps and marshes.

Lystrosaurus, which appeared as the Permian ended, was an anomodont that looked something like a hippopotamus, and even lived like one. Its eyes bulged from the top of its head; it had broad feet, used as paddles, and a chunky body. Its snout hooked downward, probably making it easy for the creature to root water plants from the bottoms of rivers and ponds.

Moschops was one of the biggest anomodonts, being about five feet high, with a huge, heavy head. It was related to *Lystrosaurus*. *Endothiodom* was a raccoon-sized reptile with a beaked snout. These, and many, many more plant-eating anomodonts, ranged the plains, deserts, and woodlands of the Permian, like game on the plains of East Africa today.

And just as lions, leopards, and cheetahs hunt the plant-eating mammals of the African plains, the plant-eating therapsids were stalked by their meat-eating relatives. They included some truly terrifying creatures—animals that still had the strength of repiles, but also some of the alertness and quickness of mammals. Indeed,

Moschops

of all therapids, the meat eaters were the closest to mammals, and were probably their ancestors.

The meat eaters belonged to a group called the theriodonts. They looked like reptilian versions of wolves, leopards, lions, and tigers. One of them, *Rubidgea*, was even larger than a tiger. Its skull was a foot and a half long, and it had huge canine teeth. Just like the saber-tooth cats of the ice ages, millions of years later, *Rubidgea* used its huge canines to stab through the thick skin of its plant-eating prey, such as *Moschops*. The swift, active creature known as *Lycaenops* was related to *Rubidgea*. It was the size of a wolf, but with exceedingly large canines, which it probably used on prey smaller than the animals eaten by *Rubidgea*.

It is important to remember that in no way was *Rubidgea* a saber-tooth cat, or *Lycaenops* a wolf—just that they filled much the same niches, or roles in the natural scheme of things, as the cat and wolf did at much later times.

The meat-eating therapsids were much more agile and fast moving than the old pelycosaurs such as *Dimetrodon*. That is because of another mammal-like trait that the therapsids possessed. Their legs were relatively long, and positioned almost

Lycaenops

directly under their bodies. Their elbows did not stick out sideways from the body, as in most reptiles, but were held close alongside it. And their feet pointed forward, not outward.

During the later Permian, the therapsid hunters roved the land, searching for prey, which they killed with their giant canines. Behind the canines were other teeth, much more advanced than those of other reptiles. The teeth were used to cut food into very small pieces, possibly even to chew it. Chewing, of course, makes for better digestion, which enables the body to extract more energy from food. The therapsid hunters needed considerably more energy than other types of reptiles, because they were so much more active.

About 220 million years ago, the Permian period faded into a new block of time, known as the Triassic. The climate once again became rather warm and stable, although not as much so as in the old Carboniferous. Mountains, such as the Appalachians, continued to rise. And, for reasons that remain a mystery, there was a great dying off among the species of animals that had prospered in the Permian. Many of the therapsids, dominant creatures of their time, disappeared. Gone were the large plant eaters, and most of the hunters such as the huge *Rubidgea.* But although the therapsids were fewer in the Triassic, those that survived became increasingly advanced.

A look at *Cynognathus*, a meat eater the size and build of a wolf, shows how far the therapsids had evolved from reptile toward the mammal. *Cynognathus* could have been found prowling the edges of marshes in what now is South Africa, searching for prey. The picture scientists have of *Cynognathus* today is based partly on the firm evidence of fossils, and partly on the best guesses about how it might have lived.

As it stalked and ran down its prey, *Cynognathus* looked very much like a wolf. The legs of this mammal-like reptile, which were under its body, were long and powerful. It had knifelike canines, and a long tail. *Cynognathus* may even have had external ears, whiskers, and hair. Its teeth indicate that it cut up and chewed its food quite well, and thus gained lots of energy. Perhaps this fact means that the creature needed energy to burn for body heat. No one is certain, but there is just a possibility that *Cynognathus* and the other therapsids of its day were warm-blooded. Proof for this idea could be that such therapsids lived where the temperature was quite cool, even cold, so needed to be warm-blooded to survive.

Even more important, *Cynognathus* belonged to a group of creatures, the cynodonts, that had developed the secondary palate. This structure, as mentioned earlier, is very important to mammals, because it permits their young to breathe while nursing. A mammal that is nursing from its mother can breathe through its nose, the breaths alternating with swallows of milk.

Cynognathus

Before the Triassic was over, however, even *Cynognathus* had passed from the scene. By the end of the Triassic, in fact, the only mammal-like reptiles remaining were a few small creatures the size of house cats and rats. Meanwhile, the dinosaurs had grown varied and numerous—and bigger. Early in the Triassic, the dinosaurs were small creatures that skittered about the landscape. By the end of the period, some dinosaurs had become as large or larger than today's alligators and crocodiles. The dinosaur was about to dominate the earth.

But let us return for a moment to the last little mammal-like reptiles. One group, the trilodonts, had developed in a new direction. Just as the therapsid hunters filled niches similar to those later occupied by wolves and big cats, the trilodont therapsids were very much like modern rodents. To be sure, the trilodonts were not rodents, but probably lived much the way rodents do today. This belief is based on the large, ratlike teeth the trilodonts had in the front of their jaws. The teeth were probably used for gnawing such food as seeds, nuts, and fruits.

Living with the trilodonts was another new group of small therapsids, the ictidosaurs. It was one of them, called *Diarthrognathus*, that possessed both the mammalian and the reptilian jaw joints, mentioned earlier. How do we classify such a creature? Perhaps the best way to describe *Diarthrognathus* is as a reptile just about to become a mammal.

Around the end of the Triassic period, or shortly thereafter, some therapsids, probably similar to *Diarthrognathus*, crossed the line from reptile to mammal. Such changes may have occurred a number of times, in more than one kind of therapsid. Certainly, they did not occur in all the therapsids that survived to the end of the Triassic. But eventually, there came a day when there were no more mammal-like reptiles on earth. Instead, there were mammals.

While the Dinosaurs Ruled

The rise of the reptiles began in the Permian. Throughout the Triassic, reptiles became more advanced, and branched into many new forms. Together, the Jurassic and Cretaceous periods, which followed, spanned 110 million years. And during that enormous expanse of time, the age of reptiles reached its peak.

There were reptiles everywhere—all over the land, in lakes, ponds, and streams, and in the seas. Even the air was conquered by reptiles, flying or gliding on great, leathery wings. It was a time when the reptiles achieved their greatest success at the game of life.

Powerful beasts, such as the long-necked plesiosaurs and fish-

Allosaurus

like ichthyosaurs were seagoing reptiles. Giant crocodiles inhabited the fresh waters. Pterosaurs sailed through the air. When these flying reptiles appeared early in the Jurassic, they were delicate creatures the size of small hawks. By the end of the Cretaceous, some had reached the dimensions of a modern fighter aircraft.

Of all the reptiles that lived in the Jurassic and Cretaceous, the dinosaurs were the most successful. Having originated in the Triassic, the dinosaurs took an astounding variety of shapes, and

Brachiosaurus

ranged in size from smaller than a man to true giants.

The first really huge dinosaurs appeared in the Jurassic, a time when vast shallow seas spread over much of North America and Europe. The climate was warm and balmy. Green jungles stretched almost to the poles. Slow, muddy rivers watered the landscape. Forests and swamps were broken by stretches of higher, drier ground. The monstrous *Brachiosaurus* sloshed through the swamps, its eighty-ton body supported by the water. Stretching its long neck here and there to gobble leaves from trees and

23

underwater plants from swamps, *Stegosaurus*, armored with vertical plates and huge spikes, ambled and grazed through woodlands where new trees such as conifers grew. And *Allosaurus*, the biggest meat eater of the time, prowled in search of food. Even the giant *Brachiosaurus* was its prey. Thirty feet long, standing on huge hind legs, with a gaping mouth full of teeth, *Allosaurus* was cat-quick and brutally strong.

As *Allosaurus* strode about the landscape, tiny mammals must have watched from the undergrowth and the trees, or even scampered out of the path of the terrifying predator. At a glance, these little creatures might have looked like shrews or mice, but they were more primitive in make-up. The first mammals were small secretive creatures. They kept in the background for millions of years while the reptiles flourished as never before or after.

Scientists have only a partial picture of the mammals of the Jurassic and Cretaceous. Because the early mammals were so small, they left little in the way of fossils. Most of what is known about them comes from a few skulls, pieces of bone, and, especially, teeth.

It is certain, however, that fairly early in the Jurassic, several groups of mammals scurried about the ferns and trees in the shadow of the dinosaurs. Among the largest of these early mammals were the tricodonts, about the size of a house cat. They are distinguished by the fact that the teeth in the side of their jaws, next to the cheek, had three chewing surfaces, one behind the other. That was a much better arrangement for chewing than the mammal-like reptiles possessed. Some of the other early mammals had even more efficient teeth. The symmetrodonts, for instance, had teeth with a triangular arrangement of chewing surfaces. This meant that the symmetrodonts had a little more area on which to chew than the tricodonts.

The different patterns of chewing surfaces on teeth may not seem very important. However, any slight advantage an animal has over others—even being able to chew better—can make the difference between survival and extinction. As it was, both the tricodonts and the symmetrodonts had vanished by the end of the Jurassic, while other groups with more advanced teeth continued to exist.

The multituberculates were among the groups that survived long after the Jurassic. Many of them were squirrel-like or ratlike in appearance and habits. They had chisel-type teeth in front, and teeth with several rows of chewing surfaces each in the rear of their jaws. This combination probably enabled them to crack open and then crush nuts and seeds, just as squirrels and rats do today.

Another group that survived the Jurassic, the pantotheres, merits special notice. The animals that belonged to it looked much like modern shrews, and like them lived largely on insects.

Cretaceous shrewlike mammal

However, these ancient mammals probably ate many other things as well. In the Cretaceous period, the pantotheres gave rise to two of the three groups of mammals that still exist today.

These three groups are the monotremes; the marsupials, or pouched mammals; and the placental mammals. The only living monotremes are the platypus and the echidna, or spiny anteater. They are very primitive. In fact, they still have a link with the reptiles, for their young hatch from eggs with white, leathery shells. Of all the mammals, they are the only ones not born alive. The origin of the monotremes is lost in time. No one knows what their ancestors were like, but because they still lay eggs, it is certain that the monotremes have existed for a very, very long while. They may have been the first of the three surviving groups of mammals to appear. Perhaps, when the monotremes arose, all mammals still hatched from eggs.

Scientists believe that both the marsupials and placental mammals branched off from the pantotheres at about the same time. The marsupials, however, are less advanced than their placental counterparts. Marsupials, which include such creatures as the opossum and kangaroo, bear their young at a very early stage of development. The newly born marsupial is blind, helpless, and tiny. A kangaroo as large as a man, for instance, has a baby only an inch long.

After birth, the young kangaroo must take a hazardous journey. Creeping and wriggling, clinging to the hair of its mother's abdomen, it struggles toward the pouch. If it reaches the pouch—which is not always the case—it attaches itself firmly to a nipple, and stays that way until it is a fully developed infant, which takes several months.

The young placental mammal, on the other hand, is not born until it is just about fully developed. It remains within its mother's womb for a long time, usually many months. During this period, the developing youngster receives nourishment and oxygen from its mother's bloodstream through an organ known as the placenta. When the placental mammal finally is born, it is much better able to take care of itself than the helpless newborn marsupial.

The Cretaceous period that witnessed the rise of the marsupials and placental mammals also saw the rise of a great variety of dinosaurs. *Brachiosaurus* had vanished, and with it *Allosaurus*. But other wondrous and often terrible kinds of dinosaurs had taken their places. The Cretaceous was the time of *Ankylosaurus*, a round dinosaur with an armored, spike-studded body, and a club at the end of its tail. It was also the time of *Triceratops*, the mighty, three-horned plant eater, which had a giant frill of bone, like a warrior's helmet, atop its head.

The plant eaters of the Cretaceous needed all the spikes, horns, and other protection they could get. Flesh-eating dinosaurs even more ferocious than *Allosaurus* prowled about the earth. Early in the Cretaceous, a monster called *Gorgosaurus* made an appearrance. Then, as the Cretaceous began to fade, the world knew the most terrible predator ever to live on land—the king of the ruling reptiles, *Tyrannosaurus rex*. Almost twice as big as *Allosaurus*, leaping and running after its prey on hind legs as thick as tree trunk, *Tyrannosaurus* was a frightening creature. Seen in mu-

28

Tyrannosaurus rex

Triceratops

Ankylosaurus

seums today, the towering skeletons of *Tyrannosaurus* seem to have come from another planet.

But, except for the animals, the landscape of the Cretaceous would have looked rather familiar to us. *Tyrannosaurus* strode not through a weird jungle but through an area covered by oaks and willows, dogwoods and poplars. During the Cretaceous, the modern flowering plants appeared and spread all over the earth.

Many mammals lived in the branches of the trees, unnoticed by the king dinosaur. Some looked like a cross between a reptile and a squirrel. These were the ptilodonts, among the many multituberculates that survived the Jurassic. But by the time of *Tyrannosaurus*, the multituberculates had plenty of competition from the more advanced marsupials and placental mammals.

One of the marsupials, creeping through the branches, was the opossum *Eodelphis*. He was furry, with a long scaly tail, and looked rather like the Virginia opossum of today. Grubbing for insects under fallen logs was the placental mammal *Zalambdalestes*, a relative of modern shrews and hedgehogs, which it resembled.

Such creatures took advantage of the few opportunities left vacant by the remarkably successful reptiles. Few of the reptiles, except for snakes and lizards, lived in the treetops, which were colonized by many mammals. Few reptiles ate insects, nuts, and seeds. Because the mammals were warm-blooded, moreover, they were able to cope with a wide temperature range. While some recent evidence strongly suggests that the dinosaurs also were warm-blooded, there is no question that the mammals can adjust to a much greater variety of temperatures than modern reptiles, and probably also bested the dinosaurs in this respect.

As long as the dinosaurs and other great reptiles lived, the mammals were held back from developing into very many new directions. The largest Cretaceous mammal, for instance, was no bigger than a small dog. Mammals larger than that would have been killed by the flesh-eating dinosaurs. Moreover, mammals could not compete with the dinosaurs for food—either meat or plants—and that also held down their size. The dinosaurs were not the dull, stupid creatures that many people believe. Scientists think that dinosaurs were rather alert. And unquestionably the dinosaurs were superbly suited to their way of life, with their keen senses, aggressiveness, and ability to adapt to new situations.

Yet, about 70 million years ago, the dinosaurs, and most other reptiles of the Cretaceous, perished. Why this happened is one of the greatest of all mysteries. There are many theories. Some scientists suggest that a change of climate or radiation from a solar flare—on outpouring of radiation from the sun—killed the dinosaurs. Others feel that something happened to the ability of the dinosaurs to reproduce—or even that the mammals crept out of hiding to feed upon dinosaur eggs.

Perhaps the mystery will never be solved. Whatever caused the extinction of the great ruling reptiles, however, the effect it had on the mammals is plain. It was their golden opportunity, for the death of the dinosaur and other Cretaceous reptiles left a vast number of vacancies in the natural scheme of things. These open niches were waiting to be filled.

There were niches in the sea, vacated by the plesiosaurs and ichthyosaurs. Their place would be taken by whales. The flying reptiles had left the air to the birds—and later to the bats. The birds, an offshoot of the group that included dinosaurs, are still viewed by some scientists as flying "reptiles." Forests of succulent foliage and plains of nourishing grasses awaited the development of larger plant-eating mammals. And mammalian flesh eaters would evolve to prey upon the plant eaters. The rule of the reptiles was over. That of the mammals was about to begin.

The Age of Mammals

The 70 million years that have passed since the extinction of the dinosaurs have been known as the age of mammals. Like the age of reptiles, the rule of the mammals also may someday end, but for now at least, the class of animals to which we belong dominates the world.

It was not until long after the last dinosaur died that the mammals took over full dominance of the earth. At first the mammals possessed few of the adaptations needed to live as grazers, browsers, and hunters on the level of the dinosaur. The mammal of millions of years ago were what scientists call unspecialized in their ways of life. Unlike the dinosaurs, few of the early mammals ate only meat or only plants. Most of the mammals at the dawn of the new age ate a little of everything—fruits, leaves, grasses, insects, and when they could, one another. Most of them lived in the trees or the undergrowth. Many of them looked alike—there was none of the great variety in appearance and habit that exists in the mammals today. There was little variety even in size. The largest mammal of the time was about as large as a springer spaniel.

In fact, the great extinction of the reptiles at the end of the

Terror cranes

Cretaceous left few large land animals in its wake. About the only ones remaining were snakes related to the boas and pythons, and a little later, fearsome flightless birds called terror cranes. The largest of these stood taller than an ostrich; they were the most powerful land creatures of their day. Their stubby wings flapping uselessly, the terror cranes raced over the landscape with great strides of their long, scaly legs. None of the mammals could withstand the pile-driving blows of their huge, hooked beaks and taloned feet.

Once the dinosaurs had vanished, however, the mammals had few enemies other than large snakes and giant birds. Slowly the mammals began to multiply, in kind as well as in number. Little by little, new forms of mammals arose to take up the niches that had been left vacant. Within 15 million years after the great extinction of the dinosaurs, the mammals were truly dominant.

The time that followed the Cretaceous is known as the Paleocene epoch. During this period, the climate of much of the earth was warm and wet. Jungles resembling those growing today in southern Mexico stretched far up into North America. Swamps and lakes dotted the landscape. Meanwhile, in the process known as continental drift the great land masses of the earth had spread far apart—farther than ever before, or since. This meant that the various groups of mammals living on the different continents lost touch with one another.

When groups of animals become isolated from one another, they tend to develop in widely different directions. The longer they are apart and out of contact, the more they change. It can happen to any groups of animals, on a local as well as a global scale. For instance, there are giant tortoises with shells shaped like saddles living on some of the Galapagos Islands. On other islands of the Galapagos chain are tortoises with high, dome-shaped shells. Once all the tortoises probably had domed shells, but the isolation of the different groups fostered the differences, although they still all belong to the same species. Eventually, if isolated long enough, different groups of the same species of animal can change so much that they will become an entirely separate species.

Also, animals can be helped to survive when isolated from similar creatures that become extinct elsewhere. Early in the age of mammals, for instance, the continent of Australia separated and drifted far apart from all the other land masses. Living aboard the drifting island continent were marsupials of many types that could not have withstood competition from more advanced placental mammals. But since Australia became extremely isolated before placental mammals really became established there, the marsupials survived in profusion. In other parts of the world most marsupials eventually vanished.

Australia has remained isolated. Other continents, however,

have come in and out of contact with one another as the rate of drift has changed and sea levels have risen and fallen. North and South America, for example, have been linked and separated a number of times. When mammals that had developed independently on the two continents met, they competed with one another. Some prospered. Others lost the competition and vanished. It all made for increasing variety among the mammals.

The rate at which the variation among mammals took place can be seen by comparing mammals that lived during the early Paleocene, with those that existed in the later part of the period. Many fossils of early Paleocene mammals have been found in the Rocky Mountain states, which were then covered by jungles and swamps, and shaken by the thunder of newly formed volcanoes.

Among the mammals of those ancient jungles were marsupials very much like the opossums of today. In fact, if we want a model of the earliest marsupials, it could easily be the opossum. The placental mammals that sloshed through the swamps and padded through the forests of the early Paleocene, however, were unlike any alive today. They were rather slow-witted, perhaps less intelligent than some of the dinosaurs before them. As a rule the early placental mammals had long, low bodies; long, heavy tails that were tapered like those of reptiles; and elongated heads. They walked flat-footed, on paws with five toes each. Most of them lived on a mixed diet of insects, worms, and vegetable matter, especially soft plants that they chewed to a pulp with blunt teeth in the sides of their jaws.

Some of these early mammals, however, began to show slight signs of specializing in one type of food or another. Here was the start of differences that would increase with time, and eventually produce creatures as distinct from each other as a dog and a cow. *Wortmania* was a stout, powerful mammal; as tall as a German shepherd dog, it may have begun to feed mainly on roots and bulbs early in the Paleocene. How do we know? Because fossils of this creature show that it had large tusks and strong heavy claws—the kinds of tools animals use for digging. And because it had blunt teeth in the sides of its jaws, scientists suspect that *Wortmania* dug for plant matter, which needs to be chewed, rather than for insects, which can be swallowed with little or no chewing.

Ectoconus shared the forest with *Wortmania*, and like it, probably fed mostly on plants. *Ectoconus* was about the size of an otter, but slightly taller. The claws on its paws were blunt and rather rounded, a clue to the direction the family to which *Ectoconus* belonged was heading. That family, the condylarths, is believed to have produced the first hoofed mammals before the Paleocene was over.

The condylarths were among the most common of Paleocene mammal families. They were fascinating creatures, because not

Wortmania

Ectoconus

only did many of them possess the traits that belong to plant-eating hoofed mammals but some of them also seem to have eaten quite a bit of meat. Among the flesh-eating condylarths were creatures called the arctocyonids, about the size of a small dog. They had long, sharp fangs, and the teeth in the sides of their jaws were pointed, as if for cutting meat, not grinding plants. The arctocyonids probably ate insects, fruits, and plants, too, but

39

almost certainly they stalked and killed other small mammals in long-forgotten forests.

By the end of the Paleocene, it would have been much easier to distinguish among the various types of mammals. Herds of a condylarth called *Phenacodus* trooped through forest glades. *Phenacodus* was a big creature the size of a donkey, although it had the same long head, tail, and body as earlier condylarths. The important thing about *Phenacodus* was its feet. The five toes on each foot no longer carried claws, but were instead, individual hooves. *Phenacodus* may have been the first condylarth—in fact, the first animal—to have them.

By the time *Phenacodus* appeared, so had the first mammals that can be considered meat eaters. Prowling about the edges of the *Phenacodus* herds was a squat, savage creature known as *Oxyaena*, one of a group of mammals called creodonts who ate nothing but flesh. Larger than a wildcat, *Oxyaena* probably was powerful enough to bring down a *Phenacodus*—if not an adult, certainly a young one. Other predators also lurked in the shadows, including the first members of the group called the carnivores— to which such existing flesh eaters as dogs, cats, seals, and weasels belong. The earliest carnivores, whose descendants would become the most savage mammals, were smaller than *Oxyaena*, and so hunted smaller prey.

Among the animals that the early flesh eaters hunted were the

Oxyaena

Phenacodus

very first horses. These creatures, which appeared late in the Paleocene, were only a fraction of the size of horses today. In fact, the "dawn horse," *Hyracotherium*, also known as *Eohippus*, was no larger than a jackrabbit. The dawn horses lived together in small herds that hid in the shadows of the forests, eating not grass but leaves and buds the way deer do today. It took millions

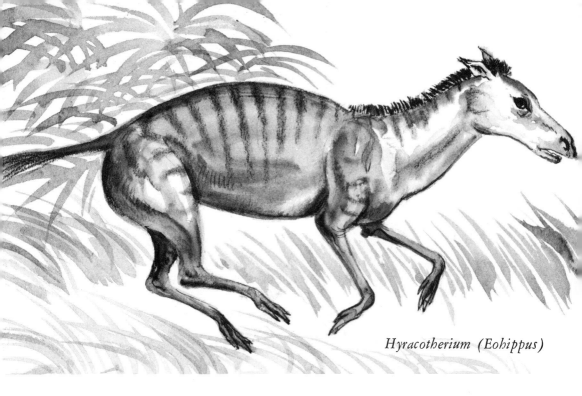

Hyracotherium (Eohippus)

of years for horses to develop the strong, powerful kinds of teeth needed for champing tough grasses.

Hyracotherium, in fact, looked a lot more like a condylarth than a modern horse. It had the same long head, and rather than walking on one large, hoofed toe like a modern horse, *Hyracotherium* darted about the forest floor on feet with several toes— four on each front foot and three on each hind foot.

As the dawn horses wandered through the vast forests, a small creature called *Paramys* scampered about the branches overhead.

It looked like a squirrel, and not by chance, for it was the first known rodent. The fact that *Paramys* and *Hyracotherium* existed before the end of the Paleocene shows that even then mammals belonging to groups still living today had already appeared. But for a long while they were strangers in a world inhabited by older, more primitive groups of mammals.

Of the primitive condylarth meat eaters, the arctocyonids died out early in the Eocene, the 20-million-year period that followed the Paleocene, but other flesh eaters continued to thrive. Some were really monstrous, such as the giant *Andrewsarchus*, which had a skull three feet long and a body bigger than a grizzly

Andrewsarchus

Uintatherium

bear's. Like the arctocyonids, however, *Andrewsarchus* probably ate vegetable matter as well as flesh. The creodonts such as *Oxyaena* were more dangerous enemies of the plant-eating animals, and during the Eocene grew as large as today's big cats.

Phenacodus survived until the middle of the Eocene. Until the early Eocene, a big primitive mammal called *Coryphodon* splashed about the rivers and lakes. It was as large as a hippo-

Coryphodon

potamus, which it resembled in appearance and habits, although the two are in no way related. Like a hippo, *Coryphodon* fed on aquatic vegetation, and defended itself with huge tusks. Another huge tusked mammal of the Eocene was *Uintatherium.* As large as a rhino, *Uintatherium* had a brain no larger than a dog's. This dull-witted beast, which fed on soft plants, carried two sets of blunt, bony horns, in addition to the swordlike tusks in its jaws.

One pair of horns was atop its head, the other on its snout. Horns and tusks probably were *Uintatherium*'s means of defense.

By the end of the Eocene, the true cats had appeared and were competing with the creodonts for prey. So were the first members of the dog family. Increasingly, animals of more modern types developed, taking over the niches of older creatures. Among the new creatures were rhinos, such as *Amynodon*, that filled the niche left by the vanished *Coryphodon*. There were also the first camels, animals on their way to becoming pigs, and pony-sized creatures with long snouts that were the ancestors of the first elephants.

Zeuglodon

In the Eocene, mammals also conquered the air and the sea. Bats similar to those of today were flitting after insects in the twilight as early as the beginning of the Eocene, 55 million years ago. And by the middle of the Eocene, whales, such as *Zeuglodon*, were chasing fish in the deeps.

The whales arose from land-living mammals whose identity is lost. Very long ago, possibly even before the Eocene, these creatures took up life at the water's edge. Perhaps they went there to avoid enemies or in search of food. At any rate, they and their descendants spent more and more time offshore. Gradually, their bodies changed. Legs were exchanged for flukes and flippers.

The body itself lengthened and became fishlike, streamlined for moving through the water. The neck shortened and jaws lengthened, making it easier to snap up fish and other aquatic prey. These mammals challenged the ancient rule of the fish in the sea.

Before the Eocene was over, the first members of most of the major groups of mammals alive today had appeared on earth. The story of the age of mammals after the Eocene is the story of the development of modern mammals. A good way to begin is with the horses that came after *Hyracotherium*.

At first these horses were not very different from the dawn horses. But they slowly changed during the following epoch, the Oligocene. Like the Eocene, this period was a time when endless forests covered the land. The horses that lived early in the Oligocene lived much as *Hyracotherium* had, quietly slipping through the woodlands to browse on shrubs and bushes. As they developed, however, they began to grow slightly in size, and some of them acquired teeth that were adapted from those needed for chopping leaves, twigs, and buds to an arrangement for grinding up tough, stringy grasses. Toward the end of the Oligocene, the climate was cooling, and a few grasslands began to appear. Some kinds of horses began to nibble grasses at the forest edge. During the Oligocene, however, horses disappeared from Eurasia, surviving only in North America.

During the next period, the Miocene, arms of grassland began to reach into forests. This encouraged the development of many new types of mammals. Grassland supports more varied kinds of mammals than deep forest. A mixture of forest and grassland provides even more possibilities for mammals to develop. As forests and grassland intermingled during the 15 million years of the Miocene, horses were one of the types of mammals that branched into several new forms.

One of these, a pony-sized creature called *Merychippus*, broke with forest life and moved out onto the grasslands. With teeth suited for grinding up grasses, *Merychippus* was able to take advantage of the vast new supply of food available on the plains. Like the horses before it, *Merychippus* was a multitoed creature, but it had three toes on each hoof. The middle toe, however, was somewhat larger than those on either side. It showed signs of developing into what we know today as the horse's hoof.

The hoof of a horse is actually the nail on an enlarged middle toe. The other toes have almost disappeared since the days of *Merychippus*, and are visible only in the horse's skeleton. A single hoof is an advantage for fast-running animals that live on the open plains, because a hoof provides more protection from stones and hard ground than a foot with many toes that spreads when weight is placed upon it. A foot that spreads gives better support

Pliohippus

on soft ground, as in marshes or on the forest floor.

The first one-hoofed horse, *Pliohippus*, appeared in the Pliocene epoch. The Pliocene had a cool, rather variable climate, which encouraged the increased invasion of grasslands into the forests. *Pliohippus* ranged over the grasslands of North America. During this period as the sea level dropped, a bridge of land eventually appeared between Alaska and Siberia. The descendants of *Pliohippus* crossed the bridge and spread over Eurasia, reestablishing the horse there. In Eurasia, horses continued to develop into the modern types. In North America, however, horses eventually vanished. Not until the Spanish explorers arrived, less than five hundred years ago, did horses again gallop on the soil of the New World.

The Pliocene horses shared the world with an astonishing variety of other mammals, many of which closely resembled their modern relatives.

The rhinos had branched out in many directions since the end of the Eocene. During the Oligocene, a hornless rhino called *Indricotherium* became the largest mammal ever to walk the earth. It was twice the size of an elephant. Another Oligocene rhino closely resembled the present-day Sumatran rhino, a medium-sized, rather hairy creature living in jungle country. In the Pliocene, rhinos close to modern types included one similar to the African black rhinoceros and another that resembled the Javan rhinoceros.

The scattered woodlands of the Pliocene teemed with deer, including kinds much like the moose and elk. Antelopes coursed over the plains of Eurasia. In North America, the huge giraffe-camel, *Alticamelus*, fed on leaves eighteen feet above the ground, and an elephantlike creature called *Gnathabelodon* scooped water plants from the mud with its spoon-shaped lower jaw.

Stalking the plant eaters were huge, savage predators. The monster hyena, *Percrocutta gigantea*, big as a lion, was the largest hyena of all time. The saber-toothed cats, which first appeared in

Gnathabelodon

Alticamelus

the Oligocene, reached the size of modern tigers in the Pliocene.
The saber-toothed *Machairodus* cats prowled both North America
and Eurasia. They killed their prey not by biting but by stabbing
with huge fangs that were so long they jutted below the lower
jaw when the mouth was closed. The first bears also were present

in both hemispheres, and foxes trotted about North America. In the Pleistocene epoch, directly after the Pliocene, the foxes crossed by the Alaskan land bridge to Eurasia.

A view of the Pliocene countryside would have shown these and many other animals, such as pigs, giraffes, beaver, porcupines, and if one looked closely on the ground, rats and mice. The old groups of mammals, which had begun to disappear as far back as the Eocene, were just about gone. A new world was dawning.

Machairodus

The Time of the Ice

This epoch was marked by titanic changes in climate. Several times great ice sheets advanced from the Arctic and from high mountains and covered immense stretches of the northern hemisphere. At one point in the Pleistocene, for instance, a sheet of ice covered North America from the polar regions to as far south as present-day New Jersey and Missouri. The ice sheets pushed animal life south. Conditions in central North America and southern Europe were like those of northern Canada and Siberia today. Animals used to the cold found new areas in which to live, but the part of the earth that could support creatures and vegetation needing a warm climate shrank.

The ice sheets, however, were not permanent. The periods of the ice, or glaciations, were separated by long stretches of time in which the world warmed. As these "interglacials" approached, the ice retreated into the north, and during this period, the ranges of cold-climate animals retreated with the ice. At the same time, warm-climate animals extended their ranges. For example, during glaciations the shaggy woolly rhinoceros, adapted to cold weather, roamed throughout southern Europe. In the interglacials, on the other hand, the woolly rhinoceros retreated far to the north, and in his place a tropical rhino similar to the modern Sumatran rhinoceros moved into Europe.

Sea levels were low during much of the Pleistocene, because so much of the water was locked in ice, and great land bridges were exposed between continents. There was a constant coming and going of animals between the great land masses. Mammals that had been isolated from one another mixed and spread over much of the world. The early Pleistocene was the time when the descendants of *Pliohippus* crossed the land bridge from North America to Asia, where they developed into modern horses. Camels also moved from North America to Asia and then on toward Africa. True elephants arose in the tropics of Africa and Asia, and spread north. In northern Europe and Asia, one branch of the elephants produced the mammoths. Some of them traveled eastward, eventually crossing the land bridge to North America.

So did bison, among the first wild cattle, which originated in Asia.

Meanwhile there also was a great exchange of mammals between North and South America, which had been linked since the Pliocene. The giant sloths, *Megatherium* and *Nothrotherium*, moved north from South America, along with armadillos, which still are extending their range in the United States. Cats, deer, tapirs, and other North American mammals went in the opposite direction.

Scientists have an exceptionally good idea of what the creatures of prehistoric North America looked like and of how they lived. This is partly because of a great trove of fossils found in the heart of the city of Los Angeles, off famous Wilshire Boulevard, in Hancock Park. It is a treasured spot of rolling green lawns, dotted with sycamores and pines, amid the concrete of the city. People flock to the park to play, sit on benches and chat, sunbathe, or just to stroll. Walking through Hancock Park, you may meet someone practicing yoga in the shade of a tree, a street musician strumming a guitar, or youngsters playing catch. It is a busy but pleasant place, one of the finest city parks anywhere. It also is one of the world's richest source of fossils of mammals from the Pleistocene epoch, the time of the great ice ages, which ended ten thousand years ago.

During the last quarter of the Pleistocene, what is now Hancock Park echoed not to the sounds of people and traffic but to the cries and roars of savage beasts. Great shaggy creatures fought and died there. Slashing, howling battles between long-gone animals were waged, often without any winner. And the bones of many of these creatures collected and fossilized in unbelievable numbers.

The reason for the large amount of fossils at Hancock Park can be seen even today. Here and there in the green grass are small pools of water and tarry, black asphalt. The asphalt formed there ages ago when oil deep in the earth began to dry out and pushed to the surface. Today the pools are known as the La Brea Tar Pits. During the Pleistocene these tar pits were a watering hole for animals. Creatures that came to the water's edge to drink were trapped in the asphalt, which clung to them in great, tarry gobs and held them helpless while they sank into the ooze. Other animals came to feed upon those that were dying in the asphalt, and they, too, were claimed by the pools. The bones of all these creatures accumulated in the pits, while the asphalt in the lower levels hardened with age. About a century ago, people found the bones, which had fossilized, and early in this century, scientists began to excavate them. The digging, which still continues today, has revealed vast amounts of knowledge about the animal life of the Pleistocene, especially in the southwestern United States.

The weather in southern California during the late Pleistocene was warm, the way it is today, because the ice sheets never reached that far south. Rain, however, was more common, and the vegetation greener. The pits shimmered in a valley floored with lush grasses and walled by cool mountains. Clumps of pine and oak dotted the valley floor, and here and there the blue-green foliage of cypress trees could be seen. Overhead circled huge birds of prey, such as giant vultures with a wingspread of twelve feet. Condors, almost as large, were ancestors of the present-day California condor. Storks, more than four feet tall, strode through the high grass, seizing lizards, frogs, and small rodents in their long bills. Red-shafted flickers and pileated woodpeckers—species still seen in the United States today—searched in dead trees for insects; and towhees rustled in the undergrowth, while up above larks and goldfinches sang in the sunlight.

Vast herds of plant-eating mammals roamed the valley around the tar pits. Massive shaggy bison, seven feet high at the shoulder, clustered together as they fed on the rich grasses. These bison were not the same type as the American bison that came later. The bison of the Pleistocene were considerably larger, with horns that measured more than eight feet from tip to tip. In the groves of trees, herds of camels nibbled on the foliage, and giant sloths pulled at the branches to bring leaves within reach of their long, curling tongues.

Now and then, trumpeting filled the air as herds of imperial and Columbian mammoths, or American mastodons, ambled toward the stream to fill their trunks with water and spray it over their mountainous bodies. And the ground thundered as groups of powerfully built horses clattered over the valley floor.

All these plant eaters were the prey of some of the most ferocious cats ever to live on earth. On the plains around what is now Hancock Park lived a gigantic cat (*Panthera atrox*), which may have been similar to a monstrous lion or perhaps a super-size jaguar. It was huge and powerful but from the look of its pony-sized skeleton very agile. The "great cat" probably hunted out in the open, stalking horses, and even the great bison, the way the African lion stalks its prey today. Slowly but surely it crept through the grass, hiding behind small bushes, until it was within several yards of its prey. Then, with an awesome burst of speed, the cat exploded from cover, hurtling over the ground on its long legs toward its prey, which it brought down with a mighty leap, a crushing bite, or possibly a slap of a massive, clawed paw.

Lurking in the brush of the valley was another large cat, every bit as frightening as the great one. It was *Smilodon*, one of the last of the saber-tooths. *Smilodon* was about the size of a lion, but built much differently. It had heavy shoulders, long and thick front legs, a barrel chest, small sloping hindquarters, and a bobtail.

Its upper jaw was armed with huge, curving fangs, longer than

Vulture

American Camel

Mastodon

Stork

a kitchen knife. Its lower jaw was rather weak and, when open, swung back as if in a monstrous yawn. There was a reason for this. *Smilodon* was not an agile creature and preyed on heavy, slow-moving creatures such as giant sloths and perhaps even adult mammoths and mastodons. When it struck, it held on to its prey with its powerful front feet, and, mouth agape, stabbed down again and again with deep thrusts of its fangs, until the prey

60

Bison

weakened and died. The nostrils of *Smilodon* were located far back atop its snout, which probably helped it to breathe when its fangs were embedded in the body of its victim.

Also roving the area were grizzly bears and a kind of bear that was even larger than the grizzlies. It was the short-faced bear, which probably fed largely on meat, rather than on a varied diet of meat, berries, fruits, and grubs as most bears do today.

There were other meat eaters around as well, including packs of the fierce dire wolves, as big as the largest living timber wolves, and pumas, closely related to those that still live on the edges of Los Angeles.

All these mammals, and many more, have been found in the tar pits. Once an animal became stuck in the asphalt, its struggles worked it even deeper into the soft, black grave. As the trapped creatures thrashed about, they bellowed and roared, which

Mastodon

brought the hungry flesh eaters. *Smilodon* regularly visited the pits to feed on trapped victims. The bones of more than two thousand of these terrible saber-toothed cats have been dug from the solidified asphalt. Dire wolves, from what the numbers of their fossils indicate, were even more numerous there.

It must have been a frightening sight, as *Smilodon*, dire wolves, and the great vultures snapped and tore at the animals caught in the asphalt. In their hunger, the flesh eaters waded out into the

Smilodon

water, and even leaped onto the bodies of the mired creatures. As the flesh eaters fed, the slick surface of the asphalt around them ballooned into glistening bubbles, which slowly bulged till they reached the size of a softball, then broke, as gas from deep within the earth surfaced and escaped. Meanwhile the flesh eaters gorged, and sometimes fought one another for their prizes. While they fed and fought, many of them were bogged down alongside their prey, and all sank to the bottom of the pits.

Day after day, year after year, century after century, the pits claimed their victims, leaving a record of the age in which lived the last of what we generally think of as "prehistoric animals." By the end of the Pleistocene, creatures such as dire wolves, saber-toothed cats, giant sloths, mammoths, mastodons, and great-horned bison had perished.

It is important, however, to remember that many kinds of mammals that lived in prehistoric days still exist. Some examples are bats, rhinos, grizzlies, and pumas. And there are many more, including giant pandas, spotted and striped hyenas, musk-oxen, and Mongolian wild horses.

Moreover, among the prehistoric mammals that survive today are not only large, exotic creatures but also smaller, more familiar ones. When *Smilodon* prowled the edges of the tar pits, for instance, gray foxes, identical to those now living in southern California, trotted through the brush. Striped skunks, no different from the kind that leave their scent in the twentieth-century night, flashed their warning when mammoths trumpeted through the valley of Los Angeles. Badgers, weasels, jackrabbits, and pocket mice lived around the ancient tar pits, and they continue to exist in California to this day. In a very real sense, we still live in a world inhabited by prehistoric creatures.

As for the mammals that vanished in the Pleistocene, ancient people painted their likenesses on cave walls, and we actually have seen a few of them in the flesh. Creatures such as woolly rhinos and mammoths have been discovered in a natural deep freeze. Their bodies, even to their shaggy hides, have been preserved in the soil of the tundra in Alaska and Siberia. The lower levels of tundra soil are frozen solid, and have been that way since the ice ages. Occasionally, when animals fell into holes in the ancient tundra, or were buried by a mud slide, and the weather was below freezing, they were completely frozen.

A number of times during this century, floods, landslides, and other natural events have uncovered the bodies of some of these ancient animals. Scientists have even been able to examine plants found in the stomachs of a few of them, indicating what sorts of things the creatures ate. Undoubtedly, many more carcasses of ice-age creatures remain locked in the Arctic deep freeze, waiting to be revealed to the eyes of humans for the first time since prehistoric people hunted them.

Ancestors and Relatives

Let us go back to the days of the king dinosaur more than 70 million years ago. In the branches of a poplar tree growing in a Cretaceous forest, a mouse-size mammal with pointed snout and long, bushy tail holds tight as its perch is shaken by the thunderous passing of *Tyrannosaurus rex*. When at last the dinosaur pushes into another part of the forest, the little mammal in the tree begins to search the foliage anew for insects to eat.

Its wide eyes bright and alert and its tail twitching, the mammal works quickly, rummaging through the leaves with deft movements of its tiny forepaws. Suddenly, it spies a cicada, and in a flash seizes the insect in one of its forepaws. The forepaw resembles a tiny hand, even though its long "fingers" are clawed. Actually, the forepaw of the little mammal is a hand in the making. The creature is one of the first primates, the group of mammals that eventually included monkeys, apes, and humans.

Very little has been discovered in the way of fossils of the earliest primates, just a tooth or two here, a jawbone there, and once in a while, a tiny skull. Yet even so, scientists have a good idea of what the first primates looked like. The few remains that have been found are similar to bones in very primitive living primates called tree shrews, which inhabit the jungles of southeast Asia.

Tree shrews, despite their name, are not really shrews, which belong to another group of mammals—the insectivores. Tree shrews have, however, some insectivore characteristics, and seem to be a bridge between the insectivores and the primates.

Scientists believe that the first primates developed from insectivores that had taken up life in the trees instead of on the ground, where most modern insectivores such as shrews and moles, live. Indeed, life in the tree is what shaped the basic body of all primates. The hand, for instance, is a direct adaptation to living in the branches. Its power to grasp was a real advantage for an animal that had to climb quickly and surely. The need to use the hands placed demands upon certain parts of the brain, which grew larger than other portions of that organ. This development led to increased intelligence. It can truly be said that all the higher primates—monkeys, apes, and even humans—evolved from adaptation to life in the trees.

Primates appeared so early that by the beginning of the Paleocene they were extremely common in many places. One group of ancient primates whose fossils are especially abundant are creatures known as *Plesiadapis*. Their fossils have been found in both North America and Europe. These creatures are particularly interesting, because in addition to being primates they also had a number of rodentlike traits. In fact, *Plesiadapis* resembled a squirrel. Some scientists believe that *Plesiadapis* was an offshoot from the main primate line, and that from this offshoot arose the rodents. This may well be true, for *Paramys*, the first rodent, resembled *Plesiadapis*, and like the primates was a tree dweller. Ironically, even to this day, primates and rodents have waged fierce competition over food and living space. Anyone who has had to worry about rats or mice in the house can vouch for this fact.

As the Eocene began, some of the tree-shrew type of primates slowly changed. Their snouts shortened, and their eyes moved from the side to the front of the snout. In that position the eyes could perceive depth more easily—another advantage for an animal that has to run and jump from branch to branch. Meanwhile, the claws on the hands and feet of most primates shortened

Plesiadapis

and flattened and became nails, which increased the ability of the primates to grasp. The creatures that resulted were animals very much like the modern lemurs, primates more primitive than monkeys, and native only to the island of Madagascar (the Malagasy Republic).

During the Eocene, as now, most lemurs were probably creatures of the night, keeping mostly to the trees but sometimes venturing down on the ground to search for fallen nuts, fruits, and grubs. Eventually, however, the lemurs branched out on their own, and developed away from the line that produced the most advanced primates, the monkeys and apes.

The first monkeys and apes seem to have appeared in the Oligocene, about 35 million years ago. The earliest monkeys were small compared to most modern monkeys. The first known monkey, called *Parapithecus*, was about the bulk of a middle-size modern monkey.

Parapithecus

Some scientists think that *Parapithecus* was more like an ape than a monkey, or perhaps that it was the ancestor of both. Such differing views are to be expected. Scientists have been able to draw the broad outlines of how groups of mammals such as the primates developed. They also have been able to sketch in the lines that branched off to form different types of primates, such as the monkeys, apes, lemurs, and others. The farther back they follow the lines, however, the more difficult it is to pinpoint individual creatures whose identities are known only on the basis of a few fossil bones. This is because the deeper into the past the lines are traced, the closer they come together, until it is often difficult to say for certain whether a creature was, for example, an ape or a monkey.

As far as the apes are concerned, their line eventually produced a creature whose fossils proclaim once and for all that it was a true ape. Scientists not only have found some of its bones, but a complete skull. This creature, *Aegyptopithecus*, lived south of modern Cairo, Egypt. In the Oligocene, the landscape was not desert, as it is now, but a lush region where low-lying, green plains met the thick tropical jungle to the south, amidst a maze of swamps and slow-moving rivers. *Aegyptopithecus* probably spent most of its time in the jungle, seldom venturing out on the plains, for it was a small tree-dwelling creature no bigger than a four-year-old child. Rather than running through the branches

Aegyptopithecus

on all fours like a monkey, however, *Aegyptopithecus* probably used its strong arms to swing about the treetops. This means of getting about aloft is one of the traits that distinguishes apes from most monkeys.

Meanwhile, monkeys continued to develop, and by the late Miocene, some types similar to living monkeys had appeared. So had a larger, heavier form of ape, *Dryopithecus*, which during the rest of the Miocene and the Pliocene spread throughout Africa and Eurasia. There were several kinds of *Dryopithecus*, some larger than others. Eventually, some types died out, but others may have led to the modern great apes, gorillas, chimpanzees, and orangutans. Of the three, only the orangutans remained primarily tree dwellers. As the grasslands pressed farther into the jungles, and the apes became bigger and better able to fight off flesh eaters, the ancestors of chimps and gorillas spent more and more time on the ground.

So did another apelike creature called *Ramapithecus*, which like *Dryopithecus*, appeared in the Miocene. *Ramapithecus* was about as large as a six-year-old human. It developed late in the

Dryopithecus

Miocene, in Africa, and in the early Pliocene spread through Europe and Asia. Most of what is known about *Ramapithecus* comes from a few pieces of jaw, facial bones, and some teeth. But these fossils tell much about the animal. Most important is the fact that *Ramapithecus* lacked large canine fangs, like those of apes and monkeys. The fangs are used by apes and monkeys for defense, to tear open thick-skinned stems and fruits, and even to kill small animals. Chimpanzees, and baboons which are really monkeys, occasionally hunt and kill other mammals such as baby antelope.

Baboons and apes also use their fangs as a warning that they have been pushed to the brink of a fight. The jaws open in a frightening yawn, and the gleaming fangs are bared for all to see. The warning may be flashed at an enemy or, more likely, at other members of an ape or monkey troop when disputes arise.

Instead of huge fangs, *Ramapithecus* had canines similar in length to its other teeth. This has greatly excited scientists, because it means that this ancient creature probably had another means of performing the tasks usually carried out by the fangs. How did *Ramapithecus* get at food surrounded by shells or tough skin? How did it warn enemies or opponents? And when necessary, how did it defend itself? The answer may be that it reached out and grabbed a rock or a stick—that it must have used tools and weapons.

74

Ramapithecus

Imagine, for a moment, the landscape of the Pliocene. Clumps of woodland dot a vast plain, where tall grasses wave in the wind. The sun is lowering. In the distance, antelope are grazing. The huge form of a rhino stands out near the horizon. At the edge of a patch of trees, a giraffe picks at leaves. Not far from the giraffe, in the shadows of the trees, a small apelike figure can be seen, but not too clearly. It seems to be standing upright, or almost so, but the shadows make it difficult to tell for sure. The creature, *Ramapithecus*, is not very large or strong compared to many of the other mammals of the grasslands, and so moves cautiously. A step at a time, its head turning nervously from side to side, it edges out of the cover of the trees, but the shadows are now so long the creature can still not be seen distinctly. Once in the tall grass, the apelike figure moves here and there, as if searching for something. Suddenly a bird flushes from the grass ahead of it. The bird flutters about, but the creature pays no attention, for it is after the bird's young, in a nest in the tall grass.

As *Ramapithecus* stoops to get at the nest, the grass behind it rustles. A hyena, one of the smaller types that lives on the grasslands, has approached. It, too, hopes to feed on the young birds. *Ramapithecus* turns to face the hyena, which has begun to snarl and bare its fangs menacingly. The hyena outweighs *Ramapithecus*, and is far more powerful. But the apelike creature seems ready to stand its ground. Quickly it reaches into the grass for something. It is a heavy stick, and *Ramapithecus* holds it aloft, waving it threateningly at the hyena. The stick can be clearly seen as *Ramapithecus* holds it ready, above its head.

This ancient use of tools—whether by *Ramapithecus* or a similar apelike primate—foreshadowed the much later accomplishments of early humans. They arose from an apelike line that, as some scientists suggest, may have included *Ramapithecus,* or at least something very similar. The use of tools grew into the making of tools, at first simple objects of bone, wood, and stone, but later devices so advanced that the primates, through their human representatives, would reach beyond the earth to the moon, planets, and stars.

For Further Reading

Bellairs, Angus d'A., *Reptiles*. London; Hutchinson and Company, 1957, 1968.

Colbert, Edwin H., *The Age of Reptiles*. New York: W. W. Norton, 1965.

Grzimke, Bernhard, *Grzimke's Animal Life Encyclopedia*, vol. 10. New York: Van Nostrand Reinhold Company, 1972.

Kurtén, Björn, *The Age of Mammals*. New York: Columbia University Press, 1972.

Pfeiffer, John E., *The Emergence of Man*. New York: Harper & Row, 1969.

Index

Italics indicate illustrations.

coal forests, 1–2, 6
competition, 36, 37, 46
condors, 58
condylarths, 38–40, 42, 43
continental drift, 35–37
Coryphodon, 44–45, 46
cotylosaurs, 7
creodonts, 40, 44, 46
Cretaceous period, 21, 22, 24, 26, 28–32, 34–35, 66
crocodilians, 7, 9, 10, 19, 22
cynodonts, 18
Cynognathus, 17–19

deer, 51, 56
Diarthrognathus, 20
Dimetrodon, 2–4, 7–8, 12, 13, 16
dinosaurs (*see also* reptiles):
    extinction of, 31–32, 34–35
    mammals and, 24, 30–31, 33–34, 66
    origin and rise of, 2, 19, 22–24, 28
dog family, 46
Dryopithecus, 72–73

echidna (spiny anteater), 26
Ectoconus, 38, 39
eggs, 31
    mammals hatched from, 26–27
    reptile vs. amphibian, 7
elephants, 5, 6, 46, 55
Endothiodom, 14
environmental changes, 17, 54–55
    adaptions and, 12–13, 31, 33
    human-caused, 4–6

Eocene epoch, 43–48, 68–69
Eodelphis, 30
Eohippus, see Hyracotherium
Eryops, 3, 7–8
evolution, process of, 12–13

fangs, 39, 59–60, 74
fossils, 13, 18, 24, 37, 38, 56–65, 67, 68, 71, 74
foxes, 53, 64

Galapagos Islands, 36
giraffes, 53
glaciations, 54–55, 58
Gnathabelodon, 51, 52
Gorgosaurus, 28
gorillas, 73
grizzly bears, 5, 6, 61, 64

hand, 66–67
hooves, 13, 40, 49
horses, 13, 41, 48, 49–51, 55, 59, 64
humans, 67, 68, 77
    impact on nature of, 4–6
hyenas, 51, 64, 76–77
Hyracotherium, 41–42, 43, 48

ice ages, 15, 54–65
ichthyosaurs, 21–22, 32
ictidosaurs, 20
Indricotherium, 51
insectivores, 67
intelligence, 67–68

interglacials, 55
isolation, 36–37, 55

jaw structure, 20
  of mammals vs. reptiles, 11–12
Jurassic period, 21, 22, 23, 24–25, 30

kangaroos, 27

La Brea Tar Pits, fossils of, 56–65
land bridges, 50, 53, 55
lemurs, 69, 71
leopards, 14, 15
lions, *10*, 14, 15, 59
lizards, 7, 30
Lycaenops, 16
Lystrosaurus, 14

Machairodus, 52, *53*
mammal-like reptiles, 8, 9, 12, 13–20, 25
mammals:
  body temperature of, 9, 30–31
  dinosaurs and, 24, 30–31, 33–34, 66
  extinctions of, 4–6, 36, 37, 64, 65
  first appearance of, 4, 24–25
  as flesh eaters, 39–40, 43, 59–64
  flesh-eating vs. plant-eating, 5, 14–15, 32, 44, 51–52, 59–61
  of Jurassic and Cretaceous periods, 24–32
  mixed diet of, 34, 37–38, 39–40, 44, 61
  modern, development of, 48–53

nursing by, 10, 18
  prehistoric, survival of, 64–65
  reptiles compared to, 8–12, 14–15
  reptilian ancestors of, 4, 7, 8, 14–15
  rise and dominance of, 33–48
  variety among, 35–37
mammoths, 55, 59, 64, 65
marsupials, 26, 27, 28, 30, 36, 37
mastodons, 59, *60–61, 62,* 64
Megatherium, 56
Merychippus, 49
Miocene epoch, 48–49, 72, 73–74
monkeys, 67, 68, 69, 70–71, 72, 74
monotremes, 26–27
Moschops, 14, 15
multituberculates, 25, 30
musk oxen, 64

niches, 16, 32
North America, prehistoric mammals of, 54–65
Nothrotherium, 56

Oligocene epoch, 48, 51, 52, 70, 71
opossums, 27, 30, 37
orangutans, 73
Oxyaena, 40, *41*, 44

palate, secondary, 10, 18
Paleocene epoch, 35–43, 68
Panthera atrox, 59
pantotheres, 25–26, 27
Paramys, 42–43, 68
Parapithecus, 70–71